1 MONTH OF
FREE
READING

at

www.ForgottenBooks.com

By purchasing this book you are eligible for one month membership to ForgottenBooks.com, giving you unlimited access to our entire collection of over 1,000,000 titles via our web site and mobile apps.

To claim your free month visit:

www.forgottenbooks.com/free1248734

ISBN 978-0-428-61011-1
PIBN 11248734

Historic, archived document

Do not assume content reflects current
scientific knowledge, policies, or practices.

THE *Fats and Oils* SITUATION

BUREAU OF AGRICULTURAL ECONOMICS
UNITED STATES DEPARTMENT OF AGRICULTURE

FOS - 104   BAE   NOVEMBER 1945

EXPORTS OF LARD FROM THE UNITED STATES, 1910-45

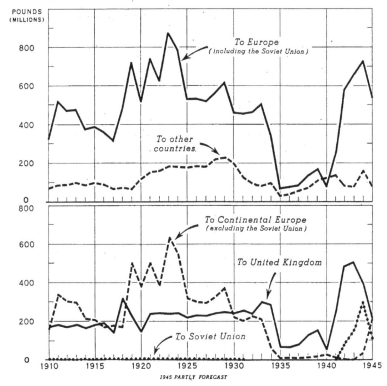

Exports of lard in 1945 (including Army procurement for European relief) probably will total 600 to 650 million pounds, compared with 886 million pounds in 1944 and 736 million pounds in 1943. In the next year or two, exports of lard probably will be smaller than in the war years, but materially larger than in the years from 1935 to 1940. In that period, drought curtailed production, and war in Europe restricted markets. Chief non-European outlets for lard are Cuba and Mexico.

Table 1.- Wholesale price per pound of fats, oils, and glycerin at specified markets, and index numbers of prices of fats and oils, October 1943 and 1944, August-October 1945

Item	PRICES				
	October		1945		
	1943	1944	August	September	October
	Cents	Cents	Cents	Cents	Cents
Butter, 92-score, Chicago	41.8	41.5	41.5	41.5	41.5
Butter, 92-score, New York	42.5	42.2	42.2	42.2	42.2
Oleomargarine, dom. veg., Chicago	19.0	19.0	19.0	19.0	19.0
Shortening containing animal fat, 1-pound cartons, Chicago	17.0	17.0	17.0	17.0	17.0
Lard, loose, Chicago	12.8	12.8	12.8	12.8	12.8
Lard, refined, tierces, Chicago	15.6	13.8	12.8	12.8	12.8
Lard, prime steam, tierces, Chicago	13.0	15.6	13.8	13.8	12.8
Lard, refined, 1-pound cartons, Chicago	10.5	13.0	15.6	15.6	13.8
Oleo oil, extra, tierces, Chicago	9.9	10.5	13.0	13.0	15.6
Oleostearine, bbl., N. Y.		9.9	10.5	10.5	13.0
Tallow, edible, Chicago				9.9	9.9
Corn oil, crude, tanks, f.o.b. mills	12.8	12.8			
Corn oil, edible, returnable drums, l.c.l., N. Y.	16.2	16.5	12.8	12.8	12.8
Cottonseed oil, crude, tanks, f.o.b., S.E. mills	12.8	12.8	16.6	16.6	16.6
Cottonseed oil, p.s.y., tank cars, N. Y.	14.0	14.3	12.8	12.8	12.8
Peanut oil, crude, tanks, f.o.b. mills	15.0	13.0	14.3	14.3	14.3
Peanut oil, refined, edible (white), drums, N. Y.	16.3	16.5	13.0	13.0	13.0
Soybean oil, crude, tank cars, midwestern mills	15.0	11.8	16.5	16.5	16.5
Soybean oil, edible, drums, l.c.l., N. Y.	14.3	15.2	11.8	11.8	11.8
Sunflower oil, semi-refined, tank cars, f.o.b. N. Y.	---	14.3	15.4	15.4	14.3
Babassu oil, tanks, N. Y.	11.0	11.1	14.3		
Coconut oil, Manila, crude, c.i.f. Pacific Coast 1/	11.8	11.0	11.1	11.1	11.1
Coconut oil, Ceylon, crude, bulk, N. Y. 1/	62.7	60.7	11.0	11.0	11.0
Olive oil, California, edible, drums, N. Y. 1/	11.4	11.4	60.7	60.7	11.8
Palm oil, Congo, crude, bulk, N. Y. 1/	2/11.5	2/11.5	11.4	11.4	60.7
Rape oil, refined, denatured, bulk, New Orleans			11.6	11.6	11.4
	8.4	8.4			11.6
Tallow, No. 1, inedible, Chicago	8.8	.8.8	8.4	8.4	8.4
Grease, A White, Chicago	8.9	8.7	8.8	8.8	8.8
Menhaden oil, crude, tanks, f.o.b. Baltimore	12.3	8.6	8.9	8.9	8.9
Sardine oil, crude, tanks, Pacific Coast	3.6	12.3	8.9	8.9	8.9
Sardine oil, refined, bleached winter, drums, N. Y.		3.6	12.3	12.3	12.3
Linseed oil foots, raw, (50% T.F.A.) delivered, East	14.5			3.6	3.6
Linseed oil, raw, tank cars, Minneapolis	15.3	14.3			
Linseed oil, raw, returnable drums, carlots, N. Y.	26.2	15.1	14.3	14.3	
Tung oil, drums, f.o.b. N. Y.	39.0	20.3	15.1	15.1	14.3
Castor oil, med. U.S.P., bbl., N. Y.		39.0	24.8	24.8	15.1
Cod oil, dehydrated, tanks, N. Y.	13.8		39.0	39.0	24.8
Cod oil, Newfoundland, drums, N. Y.	13.0	13.8	13.8		39.0
	17.7	13.0	13.0	13.8	13.8
	36.5	17.7	17.9	13.0	13.0
Soaplye, basis 80%, tanks, N. Y.	12.0	30.6	33.2	17.9	17.8
	3/11.5	17.9	11.5	33.2	33.2
		10.0		11.5	35.4
			11.1	11.3	11.7

INDEX NUMBERS (1924-29 = 100)

Item	1943	1944	August	September	October
Domestic fats and oils (1910-14 = 100)	142	142	142	142	142
Domestic fats and oils	101	101	101	101	101
...oils (27 items) origin:					
animal oils	108	108	108	108	108
oils, domestic					
oils, foreign	96	96	108	108	101
	132	96			100

1/ ...
2/ ...
3/ ...

THE *Fats and Oils* SITUATION

BUREAU OF AGRICULTURAL ECONOMICS
UNITED STATES DEPARTMENT OF·AGRICULTURE

FOS - 104   **BAE**   NOVEMBER 1945

EXPORTS OF LARD FROM THE UNITED STATES, 1910-45

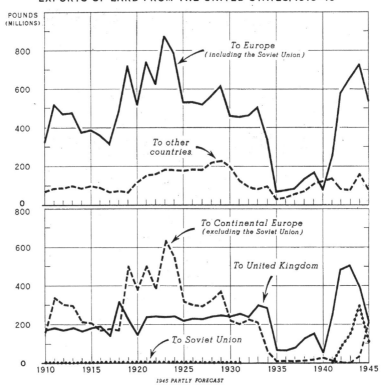

1945 PARTLY FORECAST

U. S. DEPARTMENT OF AGRICULTURE   NEG 45034   BUREAU·OF AGRICULTURAL ECONOMICS

Exports of lard in 1945 (including Army procurement for European relief) probably will total 600 to 650 million pounds, compared with 886 million pounds in 1944 and 736 million pounds in 1943. In the next year or two, exports of lard probably will be smaller than in the war years, but materially larger than in the years from 1935 to 1940. In that period, drought curtailed production, and war in Europe restricted markets. Chief non-European outlets for lard are Cuba and Mexico.

Table 1.- Wholesale price per pound of fats, oils, and glycerin at specified markets, and index
numbers of prices of fats and oils, October 1943 and 1944, August-October 1945

PRICES

Item	October 1943	October 1944	1945 August	1945 September	1945 October
	Cents	Cents	Cents	Cents	Cents
Butter, 92-score, Chicago	41.8	41.5	41.5	41.5	41.5
Butter, 92-score, New York	42.5	42.2	42.2	42.2	42.2
Oleomargarine, dom. veg., Chicago	19.0	19.0	15.0	19.0	19.0
Shortening containing animal fat, 1-pound cartons, Chicago	17.0	17.0	17.0	17.0	17.0
Lard, loose, Chicago	12.8	12.8	12.8	12.8	12.8
Lard, prime steam, tierces, Chicago	13.8	13.8	13.8	13.8	13.8
Lard, refined, 1-pound cartons, Chicago	15.6	15.6	15.6	15.6	15.6
Oleo oil, extra, tierces, Chicago	13.0	13.0	13.0	13.0	13.0
Oleostearine, bbl., N. Y.	10.5	10.5	10.5	10.5	10.5
Tallow, edible, Chicago	9.9	9.9	9.9	9.9	9.9
Corn oil, crude, tanks, f.o.b. mills	12.8	12.8	12.8	12.8	12.8
Corn oil, edible, returnable drums, l.c.l., N. Y.	16.2	16.5	16.6	16.6	16.6
Cottonseed oil, crude, tanks, f.o.b. S.E. mills	12.8	12.8	12.8	12.8	12.8
Cottonseed oil, p.s.y., tank cars, N. Y.	14.0	14.3	14.3	14.3	14.3
Peanut oil, crude, tanks, f.o.b. mills	13.0	13.0	13.0	13.0	13.0
Peanut oil, refined, edible (white), drums, N. Y.	16.3	16.5	16.5	16.5	16.5
Soybean oil, crude, tank cars, midwestern mills	11.8	11.8	11.8	11.8	11.8
Soybean oil, edible, drums, l.c.l., N. Y.	15.0	15.2	15.4	15.4	15.4
Sunflower oil, semi-refined, tank cars, f.o.b. N. Y.	14.3	14.3	14.3	14.3	14.3
Babassu oil, tanks, N. Y.	---	11.1	11.1	11.1	11.1
Coconut oil, Manila, crude, c.i.f. Pacific Coast 1/	11.0	11.0	11.0	11.0	11.0
Coconut oil, Ceylon, crude, bulk, N. Y. 1/	11.8	11.8	11.8	11.8	11.8
Olive oil, California, edible, drums, N. Y.	62.7	60.7	60.7	60.7	60.7
Palm oil, Congo, crude, bulk, N. Y. 1/	11.4	11.4	11.4	11.4	11.4
Rape oil, refined, denatured, bulk, New Orleans	2/11.5	2/11.5	11.6	11.6	11.6
Tallow, No. 1, inedible, Chicago	8.4	8.4	8.4	8.4	8.4
Grease, A White, Chicago	8.8	8.8	8.8	8.8	8.8
Menhaden oil, crude, tanks, f.o.b. Baltimore	8.9	8.7	8.9	8.9	8.9
Sardine oil, crude, tanks, Pacific Coast	8.9	8.6	8.9	8.9	8.9
Whale oil, refined, bleached winter, drums, N. Y.	12.3	12.3	12.3	12.3	12.3
Cottonseed oil foots, raw, (50% T.F.A.) delivered, East	3.6	3.6	3.6	3.6	3.6
Linseed oil, raw, tank cars, Minneapolis	14.5	14.3	14.3	14.3	14.3
Linseed oil, raw, returnable drums, carlots, N. Y.	15.3	15.1	15.1	15.1	15.1
Oiticica oil, drums, f.o.b. N. Y.	26.2	20.3	24.8	24.8	24.8
Tung oil, returnable drums, carlots, N. Y.	39.0	39.0	39.0	39.0	39.0
Castor oil, No. 3, bbl., N. Y.	13.8	13.8	13.8	13.8	13.8
Castor oil, No. 1, tanks, N. Y.	13.0	13.0	13.0	13.0	13.0
Castor oil, dehydrated, tanks, N. Y.	17.7	17.7	17.9	17.8	17.8
Cod-liver oil, med. U.S.P., bbl., N. Y.	36.5	30.6	33.2	33.2	35.4
Cod oil, Newfoundland, drums, N. Y.	12.0	11.6	11.5	11.5	11.7
Glycerin, Soaplye, basis 80%, tanks, N. Y.	3/11.5	10.0	11.1	11.3	11.5

INDEX NUMBERS (1924-29 = 100)

	October 1943	October 1944	1945 August	1945 September	1945 October
Eight domestic fats and oils (1910-14 = 100)	142	142	142	142	142
Eight domestic fats and oils	101	101	101	101	101
All fats and oils (27 items)	108	108	108	108	108
Grouped by origin:					
Animal fats	96	96	96	96	96
Marine animal oils	132	130	131	131	132
Vegetable oils, domestic	132	134	134	134	134
Vegetable oils, foreign	157	156	156	156	156
Grouped by use:					
Butter	93	93	93	93	93
Butter, seasonally adjusted	90	90	96	92	90
Lard	105	105	105	105	105
Other food fats	139	141	141	141	141
All food fats	103	103	103	103	103
Soap fats	120	120	120	120	120
Drying oils	150	149	148	148	148
Miscellaneous oils	117	116	115	115	116
All industrial fats and oils	132	131	131	131	131

Prices compiled from Oil, Paint and Drug Reporter, The National Provisioner, The Journal of Commerce (New York), and
reports of Production and Marketing Administration and Bureau of Labor Statistics. Excise taxes and duties included
where applicable. Index numbers of earlier years beginning 1910 are given in Technical Bulletin No. 757 (1940) and
The Fats and Oils Situation beginning December 1940.
1/ Three-cent processing tax added to price as originally quoted. 2/ C.i.f. New York. 3/ Drums or tanks.

EXPORTS OF LARD FROM THE UNITED STATES, 1910-45

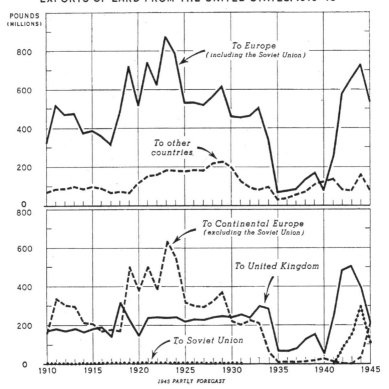

1945 PARTLY FORECAST

U. S DEPARTMENT OF AGRICULTURE   NEG 45034   BUREAU OF AGRICULTURAL ECONOMICS

Exports of lard in 1945 (including Army procurement for European relief) probably will total 600 to 650 million pounds, compared with 886 million pounds in 1944 and 736 million pounds in 1943. In the next year or two, exports of lard probably will be smaller than in the war years, but materially larger than in the years from 1935 to 1940. In that period, drought curtailed production, and war in Europe restricted markets. Chief non-European outlets for lard are Cuba and Mexico.

Item	October 1943 Cents	October 1944 Cents	1945 August Cents	1945 September Cents	Oc C
Butter, 92-score, Chicago	41.8	41.5	41.5	41.5	
Butter, 92-score, New York	42.5	42.2	42.2	42.2	
Oleomargarine, dom. veg., Chicago	19.0	19.0	19.0	19.0	
Shortening containing animal fat, 1-pound cartons, Chicago	17.0	17.0	17.0	17.0	
Lard, loose, Chicago	12.8	12.8	12.8	12.8	
Lard, prime steam, tierces, Chicago	13.8	13.8	13.8	13.8	
Lard, refined, 1-pound cartons, Chicago	15.6	15.6	15.6	15.6	
Oleo oil, extra, tierces, Chicago	13.0	13.0	13.0	13.0	
Oleostearine, bbl., N. Y.	10.5	10.5	10.5	10.5	
Tallow, edible, Chicago	9.9	9.9	9.9	9.9	
Corn oil, crude, tanks, f.o.b. mills	12.8	12.8	12.8	12.8	1
Corn oil, edible, returnable drums, l.c.l., N. Y.	16.2	16.5	16.6	16.6	1
Cottonseed oil, crude, tanks, f.o.b. S.E. mills	12.8	12.8	12.8	12.8	1:
Cottonseed oil, p.s.y., tank cars, N. Y.	14.0	14.3	14.3	14.3	1
Peanut oil, crude, tanks, f.o.b. mills	13.0	13.0	13.0	13.0	1:
Peanut oil, refined, edible (white), drums, N. Y.	16.3	16.5	16.5	16.5	16
Soybean oil, crude, tank cars, midwestern mills	11.8	11.8	11.8	11.8	11
Soybean oil, edible, drums, l.c.l., N. Y.	15.0	15.2	15.4	15.4	15
Sunflower oil, semi-refined, tank cars, f.o.b. N. Y.	14.3	14.3	14.3	14.3	14
Babassu oil, tanks, N. Y.	---	11.1	11.1	11.1	11.
Coconut oil, Manila, crude, c.i.f. Pacific Coast 1/	11.0	11.0	11.0	11.0	11.
Coconut oil, Ceylon, crude, bulk, N. Y. 1/	11.8	11.8	11.8	11.8	11.
Olive oil, California, edible, drums, N. Y.	62.7	60.7	60.7	60.7	60.
Palm oil, Congo, crude, bulk, N. Y. 1/	11.4	11.4	11.4	11.4	11.
Rape oil, refined, denatured, bulk, New Orleans	2/11.5	2/11.5	11.6	11.6	11.
Tallow, No. 1, inedible, Chicago	8.4	8.4	8.4	8.4	8.4
Grease, A White, Chicago	8.8	8.8	8.8	8.8	8.8
Menhaden oil, crude, tanks, f.o.b. Baltimore	8.9	8.7	8.9	8.9	8.9
Sardine oil, crude, tanks, Pacific Coast	8.9	8.6	8.9	8.9	8.9
Whale oil, refined, bleached winter, drums, N. Y.	12.3	12.3	12.3	12.3	12.3
Cottonseed oil foots, raw, (50% T.F.A.) delivered, East	3.6	3.6	3.6	3.6	3.6
Linseed oil, raw, tank cars, Minneapolis	14.5	14.3	14.3	14.3	14.3
Linseed oil, raw, returnable drums, carlots, N. Y.	15.3	15.1	15.1	15.1	15.1
Oiticica oil, drums, f.o.b. N. Y.	26.2	20.3	24.8	24.8	24.8
Tung oil, returnable drums, carlots, N. Y.	39.0	39.0	39.0	39.0	39.0
Castor oil, No. 3, bbl., N. Y.	13.8	13.8	13.8	13.8	13.8
Castor oil, No. 1, tanks, N. Y.	13.0	13.0	13.0	13.0	13.0
Castor oil, dehydrated, tanks, N. Y.	17.7	17.7	17.9	17.9	17.8
Cod-liver oil, med. U.S.P., bbl., N. Y.	36.5	30.6	33.2	33.2	35.4
Cod oil, Newfoundland, drums, N. Y.	12.0	11.6	11.5	11.5	11.7
Glycerin, Soaplye, basis 80%, tanks, N. Y.	3/11.5	10.0	11.1	11.3	11.5

INDEX NUMBERS (1924-29 = 100)

Eight domestic fats and oils (1910-14 = 100)	142	142	142	142	142
Eight domestic fats and oils	101	101	101	101	101
All fats and oils (27 items)	108	108	108	108	108
Grouped by origin:					
Animal fats	96	96	96	96	96
Marine animal oils	132	130	131	131	132
Vegetable oils, domestic	132	134	134	134	134
Vegetable oils, foreign	157	156	156	156	156
Grouped by use:					
Butter	93	93	93	93	93
Butter, seasonally adjusted	90	90	96	92	90
Lard	105	105	105	105	105
Other food fats	139	141	141	141	141
All food fats	103	103	103	103	103
Soap fats	120	120	120	120	120
Drying oils	150	149	148	148	148
Miscellaneous oils	117	116	115	115	116
All industrial fats and oils	132	131	131	131	131

Prices compiled from Oil, Paint and Drug Reporter, The National Provisioner, The Journal of Commerce (New York), and reports of Production and Marketing Administration and Bureau of Labor Statistics. Excise taxes and duties included where applicable. Index numbers of earlier years beginning 1910 are given in Technical Bulletin No. 737 (1940) and The Fats and Oils Situation beginning December 1940.
1/ Three-cent processing tax added to price as originally quoted. 2/ C.i.f. New York. 3/ Drums or tanks.

THE *Fats and Oils* SITUATION

BUREAU OF AGRICULTURAL ECONOMICS
UNITED STATES DEPARTMENT OF AGRICULTURE

FOS - 104   BAE   NOVEMBER 1945

EXPORTS OF LARD FROM THE UNITED STATES, 1910-45

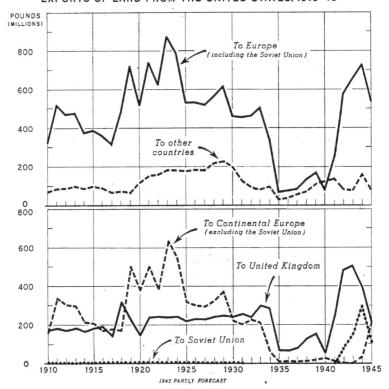

U. S DEPARTMENT OF AGRICULTURE   NEG 45034   BUREAU OF AGRICULTURAL ECONOMICS

Exports of lard in 1945 (including Army procurement for European relief) probably will total 600 to 650 million pounds, compared with 886 million pounds in 1944 and 736 million pounds in 1943. In the next year or two, exports of lard probably will be smaller than in the war years, but materially larger than in the years from 1935 to 1940. In that period, drought curtailed production, and war in Europe restricted markets. Chief non-European outlets for lard are Cuba and Mexico.

Table 1.- Wholesale price per pound of fats, oils, and glycerin at specified markets, and index
numbers of prices of fats and oils, October 1943 and 1944, August-October 1945

PRICES

Item	October		1945		
	1943	1944	August	September	October
	Cents	Cents	Cents	Cents	Cents
Butter, 92-score, Chicago	41.8	41.5	41.5	41.5	41.5
Butter, 92-score, New York	42.5	42.2	42.2	42.2	42.2
Oleomargarine, dom. veg., Chicago	19.0	19.0	19.0	19.0	19.0
Shortening containing animal fat, 1-pound cartons, Chicago	17.0	17.0	17.0	17.0	17.0
Lard, loose, Chicago	12.8	12.8	12.8	12.8	12.8
Lard, prime steam, tierces, Chicago	13.8	13.8	13.8	13.8	13.8
Lard, refined, 1-pound cartons, Chicago	15.6	15.6	15.6	15.6	15.6
Oleo oil, extra, tierces, Chicago	13.0	13.0	13.0	13.0	13.0
Oleostearine, bbl., N. Y.	10.5	10.5	10.5	10.5	10.5
Tallow, edible, Chicago	9.9	9.9	9.9	9.9	9.9
Corn oil, crude, tanks, f.o.b. mills	12.8	12.8	12.8	12.8	12.8
Corn oil, edible, returnable drums, l.c.l., N. Y.	16.2	16.5	16.6	16.6	16.6
Cottonseed oil, crude, tanks, f.o.b. S.E. mills	12.8	12.8	12.8	12.8	12.8
Cottonseed oil, p.s.y., tank cars, N. Y.	14.0	14.3	14.3	14.3	14.3
Peanut oil, crude, tanks, f.o.b. mills	13.0	13.0	13.0	13.0	13.0
Peanut oil, refined, edible (white), drums, N. Y.	16.3	16.5	16.5	16.5	16.5
Soybean oil, crude, tank cars, midwestern mills	11.8	11.8	11.8	11.8	11.8
Soybean oil, edible, drums, l.c.l., N. Y.	15.0	15.2	15.4	15.4	15.4
Sunflower oil, semi-refined, tank cars, f.o.b. N. Y.	14.3	14.3	14.3	14.3	14.3
Babassu oil, tanks, N. Y.	---	11.1	11.1	11.1	11.1
Coconut oil, Manila, crude, c.i.f. Pacific Coast 1/	11.0	11.0	11.0	11.0	11.0
Coconut oil, Ceylon, crude, bulk, N. Y. 1/	11.8	11.8	11.8	11.8	11.8
Olive oil, California, edible, drums, N. Y.	62.7	60.7	60.7	60.7	60.7
Palm oil, Congo, crude, bulk, N. Y. 1/	11.4	11.4	11.4	11.4	11.4
Rape oil, refined, denatured, bulk, New Orleans	2/11.5	2/11.5	11.6	11.6	11.6
Tallow, No. 1, inedible, Chicago	8.4	8.4	8.4	8.4	8.4
Grease, A White, Chicago	8.8	8.8	8.8	8.8	8.8
Menhaden oil, crude, tanks, f.o.b. Baltimore	8.9	8.7	8.9	8.9	8.9
Sardine oil, crude, tanks, Pacific Coast	8.9	8.6	8.9	8.9	8.9
Whale oil, refined, bleached winter, drums, N. Y.	12.3	12.3	12.3	12.3	12.3
Cottonseed oil foots, raw, (50% T.F.A.) delivered, East	3.6	3.6	3.6	3.6	3.6
Linseed oil, raw, tank cars, Minneapolis	14.6	14.3	14.3	14.3	14.3
Linseed oil, raw, returnable drums, carlots, N. Y.	15.3	15.1	15.1	15.1	15.1
Oiticica oil, drums, f.o.b. N. Y.	26.2	20.3	24.8	24.8	24.8
Tung oil, returnable drums, carlots, N. Y.	39.0	39.0	39.0	39.0	39.0
Castor oil, No. 3, bbl., N. Y.	13.8	13.8	13.8	13.8	13.8
Castor oil, No. 1, tanks, N. Y.	13.0	13.0	13.0	13.0	13.0
Castor oil, dehydrated, tanks, N. Y.	17.7	17.7	17.9	17.8	17.8
Cod-liver oil, med. U.S.P., bbl., N. Y.	36.5	30.6	33.2	33.2	36.4
Cod oil, Newfoundland, drums, N. Y.	12.0	11.6	11.5	11.5	11.7
Glycerin, Soaplye, basis 80%, tanks, N. Y.	3/11.5	10.0	11.1	11.3	11.5

INDEX NUMBERS (1924-29 = 100)

Eight domestic fats and oils (1910-14 = 100)	142	142	142	142	142
Eight domestic fats and oils	101	101	101	101	101
All fats and oils (27 items)	108	108	108	108	108
Grouped by origin:					
Animal fats	96	96	96	96	96
Marine animal oils	132	130	131	131	132
Vegetable oils, domestic	132	134	134	134	134
Vegetable oils, foreign	157	156	156	156	156
Grouped by use:					
Butter	93	93	93	93	93
Butter, seasonally adjusted	90	90	96	92	90
Lard	105	105	105	105	105
Other food fats	139	141	141	141	141
All food fats	103	103			
Soap fats					

T H.E. F A T.S ,A N D   O I L S _S.I.T.U.A T I O N

SUMMARY

Supplies of food fats for civilian consumption in the United States
in 1946 may average 44 to 45 pounds per capita,. compared with 41 to 42
pounds in 1945, an average of 48 pounds in 1936-39, and a potential demand
at the 1945 level of prices of at least 50 pounds per capita. At present
ceilings, the most pronounced shortage in food fat supplies in 1946 will be
in butter. Most of the increase in supplies in 1946 will be due to a rise
in output of lard, but a moderate expansion in butter production and declines
in exports of butter, margarine, and vegetable oils also are likely.

Production of edible vegetable oils from domestic oilseeds in 1946
may be slightly less than in 1945. Cottonseed oil production will be
unusually small in the first half of 1946, because of the small 1945 crop
of cottonseed. But in the second half of 1946 output of cottonseed oil
probably will be materially larger than a year earlier, as an increase in
cotton acreage in 1946 seems likely. Output of soybean oil in 1946 may be
slightly less than in 1945. Some increase in peanut oil production is
expected.

Soap fats probably will be in somewhat larger supply in 1946 than in 1945, as a result of moderate increases in grease production and in imports of copra. A larger supply of drying oils also will be available, reflecting the increase in the domestic crop of flaxseed in 1945, and a probable increase in imports of Argentine flaxseed and resumption of imports of Chinese tung oil in 1946. National income, though less than in 1945, will be unusually high next year. Consumer demand for fat-and-oil products will be strong. In addition, there will be a strong demand for rebuilding inventories of industrial fats and oils. Stocks of inedible tallow, grease, fish oils, linseed oil, and tung oil are now at exceptionally low levels in relation to probable use.

Returns to flaxseed producers for the 1946 crop will be supported at an average of $3.60 per bushel, Minneapolis basis, according to a recent announcement. This would be equivalent to an average of about $3.40 per bushel, farm basis. Monthly average prices to farmers for the 1945 crop, from July through October, were $2.89 per bushel. In addition, flaxseed farmers were eligible this year for special payments of $5.00 per planted acre -- equivalent to 58 cents per bushel on the basis of the national average yield per planted acre.

Subsidies to butter manufacturers were withdrawn on October 31. This was accompanied by an increase of 5 cents per pound, effective November 1, in wholesale price ceilings on butter, except butter in storage, on which the subsidy had already been paid. Butter prices advanced in November, reflecting the new ceilings. This was the first considerable increase since 1942 in the price of any leading fat or oil. Prices of other fats and oils remain at ceilings.

-- November 15, 1945

OUTLOOK

Lard Production, Domestic Consumption to Increase in 1946

Production of lard and rendered pork fat in 1946 is tentatively fore-cast at 2.4 billion pounds, 300 million pounds more than estimated output in 1945, but 800 million pounds less than the record production of 3.2 billion pounds in 1944. Hogs from the 1945 spring pig crop are being marketed later and at heavier weights than usual. This may result in a larger hog slaughter in the first 4 months of 1946 than a year earlier. The yield of lard per hog slaughtered also is likely to be larger than in early 1945, when export require-ments for fat pork cuts were unusually heavy. In May-September 1946, hog slaughter will be larger than a year earlier, reflecting an increase in the number of sows farrowed in the 1945 fall season. Lard output in October - December next year may be at least as large as in the corresponding months of 1945. Hog slaughter in the last 3 months of 1946 will be chiefly from the 1946 spring pig crop. A spring pig crop goal of 52 million head, the same as the number saved in the spring season of 1945, recently was announced by the Department of Agriculture.

Lard exports in 1946 probably will be smaller than the total of 600 to 650 million pounds in 1945, but will be materially larger than in the years just before the war. From 1935 to 1940, lard exports from the United States were severely curtailed, as a result of droughts and by war in Europe. Annual average exports in 1935-40 were 172 million pounds, compared with 561 million pounds in 1930-34. In 1946, with world supplies of fats and oils still short, there will be a strong European demand for United States lard.

Since World War I, the principal markets for United States lard have been the United Kingdom, Germany, other Western European countries, and Latin America. For many years prior to 1934, a year of severe drought followed by reduced lard output, the United Kingdom took a relatively stable quantity of United States lard, with shipments averaging 262 million pounds annually in 1930-34. In 1942-44, exports of lard to the United Kingdom averaged 461 million pounds annually, but this quantity probably will be substantially reduced in the next few years. Continental Europe, chiefly Germany, was the largest importer of United States lard in the early and middle 1920's, but in 1930-34 imports declined to an average of only 182 million pounds. In 1946, the countries of western Europe will take at least as much as in 1945 — 150 to 200 million pounds. Exports to Latin American countries in 1942-44 averaged 99 million pounds annually, compared with 110 million pounds in 1930-34. This market probably will continue to take about 100 million pounds a year. Around 35 million pounds of lard are shipped annually to the territorial possessions of the United States.

A large quantity of lard was shipped under lend-lease to the Soviet Union during the war, with a peak of 294 million pounds in 1944. But it does not seem probable that the Soviet Union will be a major market for United States lard after immediate relief needs are met.

Table 2.- Lard: Exports to specified countries, and shipments to
United States territories,1930-34 and 1942-45

Destination	Average 1930-34	1942	1943	1944	January-August 1945
	Mil. lb.	Mil. lb.	Mil. lb.	Mil. lb.	Mil. lb.
Exports:					
United Kingdom ...:	261.5	485.1	504.4	393.9	146.0
Germany ....:	112.1	---	---	---	---
Continental Europe:					
excluding Germany:					
and the Soviet Union:	69.6	.5	.8	10.1	135.1
Soviet Union .....:	1/	88.2	155.5	293.9	105.2
Other countries ..:	117.9	77.8	75.6	160.9	57.6
Total ....:	561.1	651.6	736.4	858.8	443.9
Shipments to U.S. :					
territories ......:	23.0	32.8	38.9	35.6	21.2
Total exports and :					
shipments........:	584.1	684.4	775.3	894.4	465.1

Compiled from official records of the Bureau of the Census, except that
shipments to territories include quantities shipped under special programs
of the U. S. Department of Agriculture, reported by USDA. Totals computed from
unrounded numbers. 1/ Less than 50,000 pounds.

Assuming exports of 500 to 600 million pounds of lard in 1946 and use
of 55 million pounds in margarine and shortening (the average of recent years),
the balance available for total civilian and military use as lard would be
1,8000 to 1,350 million pounds. This would be about 13 pounds per capita, compared with an estimated domestic consumption of 11.7 pounds per capita in 1945,
and a long-time average (except the drought period) of 13 to 14 pounds per capita.

Slight Decrease Likely in Production of Edible Vegetable Oils in 1946

Total production of edible vegetable oils from domestic oilseeds in
1946 may be slightly less than in 1945. Output of cottonseed oil in the
first half of 1946 will be materially smaller than a year earlier, as a
result of the reduced 1945 crop of cottonseed. However, if cotton acreage
were increased in 1946 to a level near that in the years just before the
war, cottonseed oil production in the latter half of 1946 would be substantially larger than the unusually low output in the corresponding period
of 1945. The total for the year may be slightly smaller than the total in
1945.

Production of soybean oil in 1946 may be slightly smaller than in 1945.
With a slight reduction indicated in the 1945 crop of soybeans and with a
strong export demand for soybeans, crushings in January-September 1946 are
likely to be a little smaller than a year earlier. Also, a reduction in
soybean acreage is probable in 1946 as a result of shifts to hay and pasture.
This would mean a slightly smaller soybean-oil output in October-December 1946
than in October-December 1945. Crushings of peanuts and production of peanut
oil in 1946 probably will be somewhat greater than a year earlier, as a result
of an increase in the 1945 crop of peanuts and a reduction in miliary requirements for shelled peanut products.

Butter Production, Domestic Consumption
  Up Moderately in 1946

      Butter production is expected to be slightly larger in 1946 than
the 1,720 million pounds estimated for 1945, with the increase coming in the
season of flush production and later. Production is likely to remain below the
level of a year earlier during the first 3 months of 1946, unless butter prices
rise above present levels. Exports of butter in 1946 including shipments to
United States territories, are expected to return to the prewar level of about
10 million pounds. In 1945, around 30 million pounds of butter have been
exported, with approximately 25 million pounds (including butter oil and Carter
spread) going under lend-lease to the Russian Army. Domestic supplies of butter
in 1946 may be moderately larger than in 1945. Also, reduced military procurement will add to civilian supplies per capita. Military takings of butter
during the war were more than twice as large, on a per capita basis, as civilian
supplies. The civilian supply per capita in 1946 will still be materially less
than prewar.

Civilian Supply of Food Fats to Increase in
  1946 But Likely to Remain Short of Demand

      Present prospects for 1946 indicate a civilian supply of 44 to 45
pounds of food fats and oils per capita, including butter in terms of actual
weight. This is comparable with an estimate of 41 to 42 pounds per capita
in 1945 and a 1935-39 average of 48 pounds per capita. With national income
expected to be at a high level in 1946, consumer demand for food fats and oils
probably will be strong enough to support a consumption of at least 50 pounds
per capita, with prices at present levels. This demand will keep prices of
food fats and oils at ceiling levels in 1946. If ceilings are raised or
removed, prices of food fats will advance. With a continuation of present
prices, the gap between demand and supply probably will be narrower after mid-
1946 than in the first part of the year, principally because of increased
output of cottonseed oil and butter in relation to corresponding months of 1945.

Soap Fat Situation To Improve in 1946

      Supplies of soap fats probably will increase in 1946. With hog
slaughter expected to be larger than in 1946, output of grease is likely to
increase moderately. Also, fairly substantial imports of Philippine copra
are expected in 1946. However, imports of coconut oil and copra from Ceylon
and the South Sea islands, which approached 200 million pounds annually (in
terms of oil) in 1944 and 1945, will be severely curtailed in 1946. Total
imports of coconut oil and copra (in terms of oil) probably will be less than
half as large as the 1937-41 average of 700 million pounds.

      Military procurement of soap fats will be substantially reduced in 1946.
For 1945 as a whole, military takings of soap will total around 300 million
pounds in terms of fat (preliminary) out of a total soap production for all
purposes of about 2,100 million pounds, in terms of fat content.

      Demand for soap fats will be strengthened during 1946 by the need to
rebuild inventories of inedible tallow, grease, and fish oils. These inventories are now materially below normal.

Increase in Supplies of Drying Oils in 1946
Dependent on Imports

Supplies of linseed oil continue short of demand at ceiling prices, despite peak-season crushing of the relatively large 1945 domestic crop of flaxseed. Many Eastern seaboard mills, which depend largely on Argentine flaxseed, were closed from midsummer until recently. However, recent receipts at these mills of some domestic and Argentine flaxseed have permitted resumption of crushing on a limited scale.

Relief of the tightness in linseed-oil supplies will depend on arrival of Argentine flaxseed in volume. The 1945-46 Argentine crop, to be harvested beginning in December, is expected to be smaller than average but substantially larger than the 1944-45 crop. However, European demand for Argentine flaxseed is strong. United States supplies of drying oils in 1946 will be increased by resumption of imports of tung oil from China.

Reduction in military requirements for drying-oil products has already permitted a substantial increase in use of such oils in civilian products from the unusually low level of mid-1945.

Stocks of drying oils on September 1 were at an exceptionally low level. Demand for oil to rebuild inventories will be an important part of the total demand for drying oils in 1946.

Returns per Bushel for 1946 Flaxseed
To Be Supported at $3.60
Minneapolis Basis

It was announced on November 8 that returns to growers for flaxseed harvested in 1946 will be supported, by acreage payments or otherwise, at an average level equivalent to $3.60 per bushel, Minneapolis basis. This would mean a national season average return to farmers in 1946-47 of about $3.40 per bushel (farm basis), compared with an average price of $2.89 per bushel in July-October 1945, plus a payment of $5.00 per planted acre, equivalent to 58 cents per bushel on the basis of the national average yield of 8.6 bushels per planted acre in 1945. Farmers who planted flaxseed in 1945 up to their farm acreage goals were eligible for the payment of $5.00 per acre.

Planted acreage of flaxseed in the United States for harvest in 1945 was 4.1 million acres compared with 3.1 million acres a year earlier. Prices to farmers were approximately the same for both crops, but in 1945 the additional payment of $5.00 per acre was offered. With a high average return per bushel guaranteed for the 1946 crop, planted acreage is likely to be maintained at a high level next season.

A strong demand for linseed oil is anticipated in 1946-47, on the basis of a high rate of industrial production and a return of building activity to a relatively high level.

RECENT DEVELOPMENTS

Deterioration in Oilseed-Crop Prospects During October

Heavy rains and cold weather in Texas, Oklahoma, and Arkansas in early October reduced the late cotton crop and caused some damage to peanuts still in the ground and to those dug but not yet threshed. On the basis of November 1 conditions, production of cottonseed this year would be 3,858,000 tons, assuming the 1940-44 average ratio between yields of lint and seed. The 1944 production of cottonseed was 4,901,000 tons. The 1945 output of peanuts picked and threshed is now placed at 2,174 million pounds, compared with 2,260 million pounds indicated on October 1, and with a 1944 crop of 2,111 million pounds.

Harvesting of soybeans, which began in October, revealed less well-filled pods and smaller beans than had been expected. As a result, the November 1 indication for the 1945 soybean crop is 191 million bushels, 6 million bushels less than indicated a month earlier, and 2 million bushels less than the 1944 crop.

Table 3.- Oilseeds: Yield per acre and production, 1943-45

Commodity		Yield per acre 1/				Production		
	Unit	1943	1944	Indi-cated 1945	Unit	1943	1944	Indi-cated 1945
Soybeans	Bu.	18.1	18.4	18.0	Mil. bu.	193.1	192.9	190.6
Flaxseed	"	8.2	7.7	8.6	"	51.9	23.5	35.6
Cottonseed	Lb.	427	482	420	1,000 tons	4,688	4,901	3,858
Peanuts	"	608	670	672	Mil. lb.	2,185	2,111	2,174

1/ Soybeans, per acre harvested for beans; flaxseed, per planted acre; cottonseed, per acre in cultivation July 1; peanuts, per acre picked and threshed.

World Peanut Production Slightly Increased in 1945

Preliminary estimates indicate that world peanut production in 1945 may be about 20.1 billion pounds, 0.4 billion pounds more than in 1944 and 1.5 billion pounds more than in 1935-39. A large part of the increase over 1944 is in Senegal, the leading peanut-producing section of French West Africa, where a crop of 772 million pounds is indicated, 270 million pounds more than were harvested a year earlier.

The indicated United States crop of 2,174 million pounds is about 60 million pounds larger than in 1944.

No reports have yet been received on production in India and China, but total output in Asia is provisionally estimated at 15.0 billion pounds,

about the same as last year. India, French West Africa, Nigeria (Part of
British West Africa), and China were the principal exporters of peanuts and
peanut oil before the war.

Table 4. - World peanut production, average 1935-39, annual 1944 and 1945

Continent and country	Average 1935-39	1944	Preliminary, 1945
	Mil. lb.	Mil. lb.	Mil. lb.
North America			
United States	1,229	2,111	1/ 2,174
Estimated total	1,279	2,285	1/ 2,360
Europe, estimated total	83	87	87
Asia			
India	6,591	7,974	N. A.
China	5,379	2/2,400	N. A.
Estimated total	13,636	14,946	15,000
Africa			
French West Africa	1,752	551	1/ 3/ 900
Nigeria	4/ 676	4/ 612	4/ 616
Estimated total	3,305	1,809	2/ 2,100
South America			
Argentina	175	438	349
Estimated total	257	548	500
Oceania (including Australia)			
Estimated total	13	18	19
Estimated world total	18,573	19,693	1/20,100

Office of Foreign Agricultural Relations (Foreign Crops and Markets, 51:17;230
October 22, 1945).
1/ Revised. 2/ Free China only. 3/ Unofficial estimate. 4/ Production not
available; exports are shown.

World Flaxseed Output Up in 1945

World flaxseed production in 1945 (including Southern Hemisphere crops
partly harvested in 1946) may total about 150 million bushels, according to
latest indications. This is 26 million bushels more than last year and 13
million bushels more than the 1935-39 average. The United States crop this
year is estimated at 35.6 million bushels, 12.1 million bushels more than
last year. No official estimate of the Argentine crop, to be harvested
beginning in December, has yet been made. About 4.6 million acres were
planted this year, 2 percent less than in 1944. But unusually favorable
weather since planting time is expected to result in a substantially larger
output this year than in 1944-45, when yields were severely reduced by
drought. Output of flaxseed in India in 1945 is placed at 15.6 million
bushels, compared with 15.2 million bushels last year.

Table 5.- World production of flaxseed (China excluded), average 1935-39,
annual 1944 and 1945

Continent and country	Average :1935-39	1944	Preliminary : 1945
	Mil. bu.	Mil. bu.	Mil. bu.
North America			
United States	11.0	23.5	1/35.6
Canada	1.5	9.7	7.4
Mexico	.1	2/1.0	2/ 1.2
Estimated total	12.7	34.3	1/44.3
Europe, excluding the Soviet Union			
Estimated total	9.4	10.3	7.5
Soviet Union	3/29.5	N. A.	N. A.
Asia			
India	18.1	15.2	15.6
Estimated total, excluding China	20.4	17.0	16.2
Africa			
Estimated total	.5	.7	.3
South America			
Argentina	59.6	31.0	N. A.
Uruguay	3.9	1/ 3.9	N. A.
Estimated Total	64.2	1/35.6	54.0
Oceania (including Australia)			
Estimated total	---	.2	.2
Estimated world total, excluding China:	136.8	124.0	1/150.6

Office of Foreign Agricultural Relations (Foreign Crops and Markets,
51:13:174; September 24, 1945).
1/ Revised.
2/ Unofficial estimate.
3/ Average of less than 5 years.

GOVERNMENT ACTIONS

Ceiling Prices Established for Soybeans
Produced in 1945

Maximum Price Regulation 600, effective November 2, established maximum
prices for 1945-crop soybeans at the same levels as those formerly in effect
under MPR 573 for soybeans produced in 1944. The ceiling for producers' bulk
sales of U. S. No. 2 green or yellow soybeans is $2.10 per bushel. However,
soybeans to be used for planting in 1946 and soybeans especially cleaned for
use in food products are exempt from price ceilings. The support price to
producers this season for No. 1 or No. 2 green or yellow soybeans is $2.04
per bushel, the same as in 1944-45.

Butter Subsidy and "Roll-Back"
Terminated

The Government subsidy of 5 cents per pound to butter manufacturers,
in effect since June 1, 1943, was ended October 31, 1945. On November 1,
ceiling prices for sales of unsubsidized butter by manufacturers and wholesalers were raised 5 cents per pound by Amendment 39 to Revised Maximum Price

Regulation 289. The new ceiling for manufacturers' sales of bulk 92-score butter, delivered at Chicago, is 46 cents per pound. Regulations governing retail mark-ups permit increases averaging 5 to 6 cents in the retail price per pound of unsubsidized butter. The new retail price ceilings also became effective November 1. Stored butter on which the subsidy had already been paid remains subject to the old ceilings unless 5 cents per pound is returned to the Treasury. The average retail price of butter in leading cities in recent months prior to November was 50 cents per pound.

These increases in ceiling prices will allow butter prices to rise to approximately the levels prevailing in May 1943. Butter ceilings were reduced in June 1943 as part of the program to hold the cost of living in check.

Peanut Butter Subsidy Ended;
Price Ceilings Increased

Subsidy payments by Commodity Credit Corporation to peanut butter manufacturers were ended October 31. These payments had been made at the rate of 4.5 cents per pound from November 1, 1943 to August 31, 1945, and at the rate of 4.0 cents per pound from September 1, 1945 to October 31, 1945. Payments had been made only on peanut butter packed in retail-size containers (2 pounds or less).

Manufacturers' ceiling prices for peanut butter packed in retail containers were raised 4 cents per pound on November 1 by Amendment 1 to RMPR 435. This action was taken to compensate manufactueres for withdrawal of the subsidy. Under regulations governing wholesale and retail price ceilings, retail prices of peanut butter may advance approximately 6 cents per pound when the 4-cent increase in processors' ceiling is fully reflected. The average retail price of peanut butter in recent months in leading cities of the United States was 23.6 cents per pound.

Shortening Subsidy To Be Terminated

It was announced in November that shortening subsidies would be terminated on or before December 31, 1945. Under the present program, in effect since mid-December 1943, shortening manufacturers are eligible for payments from Commodity Credit Corporation on shortening sold to wholesalers, retailers, or consumers and sold in drums or tierces. The rate of payment is 0.2 cent per pound on the vegetable-oil content of hydrogenated shortening and 1.4 cent per pound on the vegetable-oil content of standard shortening.

Specific Maximums Established for
Olive Oil "Foots"

Amendment 51 to Maximum Price Regulation 53, effective October 22, established specific maximum prices for olive oil "foots" (sulfur olive oil) at 17 cents per pound. This maximum applies to domestic oil in tank cars, f.o.b. seller's plant, and to imported oil in tank cars, f.o.b. port of entry. An additional cent per pound may be charged for oil sold in drums. Olive oil "foots" is an inedible oil extracted from olive press cake residue by use of solvents, and is used mainly in soap manufacture.

Set-Aside Percentage Reduced
For Lard

The quantity of lard that federally inspected packers in 19 States are required to set aside for purchase by Government agencies was reduced on November 4 from 4 percent to 3 1/2 percent of the total live weight of hogs slaughtered. This action was taken in Amendment 24 to War Food Order 75.3. The States in which this requirement is effective are Ohio, Indiana, Illinois, Michigan, Wisconsin, Minnesota, North Dakota, South Dakota, Iowa, Nebraska, Kansas, Missouri, Montana, Idaho, Wyoming, Colorado, Nevada, New Mexico, and Arizona. The set-aside is equivalent to 20 to 25 percent of total output of federally inspected lard and rendered pork fat.

Use Preference for Inedible Tallow
and Grease Removed

War Food Order 67 was amended, effective October 1, to revoke provisions requiring priority to be given orders for inedible tallow and grease for use in non-soap products. All users may now purchase inedible tallow and grease on an equal basis, subject only to the inventory restrictions of the order, which remains in force.

Restrictions on Use of Rapeseed Oil
Terminated

War Food Order 35, limiting the use of rapeseed and mustardseed oils to the manufacture of war products, mainly marine engine lubricants, was terminated November 1. With Government requirements for these oils sharply reduced, restrictions on their use were no longer necessary.

Correction

Private imports of edible and inedible tallows continued subject to controls under WFO 63 from July 20 to September 20, 1945 and still are controlled. In the October issue of The Fats and Oils Situation (page 18) it was erroneously stated that tallow had been exempted from WFO 63 by Amendment 3, effective July 20, but restored to control by Amendment 5, effective September 20.

Table 6.- Supply and disposition of fats and oils, average 1937-41, Annual 1942-45

Item	Average 1937-41	1942	1943	1944	1945 1/
	Bil. lb.	Bil. lb.	Bil. lb.	Bil. lb.	Bil. lb.
Production from domestic materials					
Butter: Creamery	1.780	1.764	1.674	1.487	
Farm	.431	.366	.341	.329	
Total	2.211	2.130	2.015	1.816	1.720
Lard and rendered pork fat:					
Inspected	1.224	1.724	2.080	2.367	
Other	.740	.745	.977	.848	
Total	1.964	2.469	3.056	3.215	2.100
Edible tallow, oleostearine, oleo stock, and oleo oil	.213	.277	.259	.198	.220
Corn oil	.155	.248	.237	.211	.220
Cottonseed oil	1.472	1.386	1.313	1.132	1.240
Peanut oil	.087	.077	.153 2/	.108 2/	.100
Soybean oil	.413	.762	1.234	1.246	1.320
Inedible tallow and greases	1.167	1.742	1.650	1.943	1.750
Marine animal oils	.243	.158	.175	.215	.210
Linseed oil 3/	.277	.699	.715	.729	.450
Other	.021	.035	.040	.037	.040
Total, from domestic materials	8.230	9.983	10.848	10.849	9.370
Stocks, January 1 (crude basis)	2.2	2.3	2.0	2.2	2.2
Imports of oil and factory production of oil from imported materials 4/	2.0	1.0	.9	1.0	.8
Total supply	12.4	13.3	13.8	14.0	12.4
Exports, reexports and Shipments					
To U. S. terrotories 4/	.4	.9	1.6	1.6	1.1
Stocks, December 31 (crude basis)	2.3	2.0	2.2	2.2	1.7
Domestic disappearance	9.7	10.3	10.0	10.2	9.6
Military procurement, excl. relief	---	.5	.9	1.1	1.1
Estimated civilian disappearance	9.7	9.8	9.1	9.1	8.5
	Pounds	Pounds	Pounds	Pounds	Pounds
Civilian disappearance, per capita	74	74	70	70	65

Compiled from reports of the Bureau of the Census, Fish and Wildlife Service and U. S. Department of Agriculture. Totals computed from unrounded numbers.
1/ Partly forecast.
2/ Total production minus oil equivalent of imported Argentine peanuts.
3/ Total production minus oil equivalent of net imports of flaxseed.
4/ Imports include shortening and soap in terms of fat content. Exports include margarine, shortening, and soap in terms of fat content, procurement by the Army for European relief and procurement by the American Red Cross. Exports do not include oil equivalent of oilseeds exported.

Table 7.- Imports and exports of fats, oils, oil-bearing materials, and fat-and-oil products, January-August, average 1938-41, 1944 and 1945

Primary fats

Item	Imports for consumption			Exports 1/		
	Average 1938-41	1944	1945 2/	Average 1938-41	1944	1945 2/
	Mil. lb.	Mil. lb.	Mil. lb.	Mil. lb.	Mil. lb.	Mil. lb.
Animal fats						
Butter	1.1	1.7	3/	6.4	50.8	4/ 23.9
Lard	3/	3/	.2	151.6	617.1	455.1
Oleo oil	---	---	---	2.3	2.4	.2
Stearine, animal, adiola	3/		.2	.1	---	3/
Oleo stock	---	---	---	1.6	.2	---
Tallow, edible	.6	18.8	1.7	.1	1.1	3/
Tallow, inedible	.3.9	37.5	31.6	1.0	14.6	4.4
Greases	3/	3/	3/	2.7	1.9	4.3
Wool grease	1.6	3/	.6	---	---	---
Neat's-foot oil	---	.4	.6	.4	.1	.1
Total, animal	7.2	56.4	34.9	206.3	688.2	504.0
Marine fats						
Fish-liver oils	27.2	15.6	14.5	---	1.2	3.0
Fish oils	1.6	8.6	10.2	2.1	7.4	8.2
Marine mammal oils	14.2	1.5	1.9	3/	2.7	13.0
Total, marine	43.0	25.7	26.7	2.1	11.4	24.2
Vegetable fats						
Babassu oil	.3	.9	2.7	---	---	---
Cashew nut shell liquid (oil)	2.0	4.2	.2	---	---	---
Castor oil	.1	15.6	7.1	.7	1.7	.9
Coconut oil	242.2	37.3	30.7	24.1	4.9	.1
Corn oil	7.4	3/	3/	.1	.2	.1
Cottonseed oil	24.3	4.6	33.0	7.4	4.3	7.0
Japan wax (tallow)	1.7	---	---	---	---	---
Linseed oil	.1	63.9	29.3	1.9	237.6	6.4
Oiticica oil	13.6	6.0	15.1	---	---	---
Olive oil, edible	36.0	.2	8.7	---	.1	.1
Olive-oil "foots"	14.3	---	---	---	.4	.1
Olive oil, inedible	3.3	.1	.1	---	3/	3/
Palm-kernel oil	1.1	---	---	---	---	---
Palm oil	180.5	39.9	331.9	12.2	4.2	14.6
Peanut oil	3.3	3/	---	2.0	.2	.1
Perilla oil	16.2	---	---	---	3/	---
Rape oil	7.1	13.0	17.7	---	.2	.5
Sesame oil	2.2	.9	---	---	---	---
Soybean oil	1.9	.1	---	7.7	33.1	28.4
Sunflower oil	.1	33.2	57.6	5/	5/	39.0
Teaseed oil	3.2	---	---	---	---	---
Tung oil	59.3	1.8	.2	2.9	.1	1.5
Vegetable tallow	1.1	3/	.3	---	---	---
Other vegetable oils and fats	---	1.0	1.1	6/10.2	10.4	2.1
Vegetable oils, shipments to U. S. territories	---	1.1	---	6/ 6.2	5.5	5.0
Total, vegetable	621.2	219.7	282.1	75.5	333.0	155.9
Total, primary fats	671.4	303.9	313.7	283.9	1,032.5	654.1
Oil-bearing materials (in terms of oil)						
Babassu kernels (63 percent)	37.5	4.8	33.5	---	---	---
Castor beans (45 percent)	64.7	104.2	97.7	---	---	---
Copra (63 percent)	219.1	75.2	114.0	14.8	---	---
Cottonseed (15.5 percent)	---	---	3/	---	.5	1.0
Flaxseed (34 percent)	198.7	173.0	63.2	---	.3	3/
Murumuru kernels (36 percent) 7/	.9	.4	.3	---	---	---
Palm-nut kernels (45 percent)	6.0	8.8	36.3	---	---	---
Peanuts, snelled (39 percent)	---	---	15.6	---	---	---
Perilla seed (37 percent)	.6	---	---	---	---	---
Sesame seed (47 percent)	3.1	3.4	3/	---	---	---
Soybeans (15 percent)	---	---	---	9.9	3.5	38.3
Tucum kernels (43 percent)	2.4	.7	3.9	---	---	---
Total, oil-bearing materials	533.0	370.5	368.5	23.7	4.4	39.3
Manufactured products (fat content)						
Margarine 8/	6/ 1.2	---	---	6/ 1.0	41.9	44.9
Shortening	6/ .5	3/	3/	6/ 5.6	10.4	15.9
Soap	6/ 2.0	.3	.2	6/20.9	20.5	37.1
Total, manufactured products	4.1	.3	.2	27.5	72.7	97.9
Grand total						
All items	1,208.4	674.6	672.5	335.1	1,079.6	771.3

Compiled from Monthly Summary of Foreign Commerce of the United States, records of the Bureau of the Census, and reports of the U. S. Department of Agriculture. Totals computed from unrounded numbers.

The following items are not included above: Procurement by the Army in 1945 for European relief, 65 million pounds of lard and 6 million pounce fat content of soap. Procurement of margarine, shortening, and soap by the American Red Cross, in terms of fat content, 14 million pounds in 1944 and 10 million pounce in 1945.

1/ Includes shipments to U. S. territories of butter, lard, and manufactured products; reexports of coconut, palm, and tung oils, olive-oil foots, and copra; and reexports in 1944 and 1945 of certain quantities of whale oil and sunflower oil reported in imports for consumption. Shipments include special programs of USLA in 1944 and 1945. 2/ Preliminary. 3/ Less than 50,000 pounds. 4/ Includes actual weight of butter oil and spreads (Army). These were not reported separately prior to 1945. 5/ Not reported separately. 6/ Eight-twelfths of annual average. 7/ 1938-41, 35 percent. 8/ Imported margarine goes largely to Puerto Rico and the Virgin Islands.

Table 8.-Fats and oils: Total factory production, January-August 1944 and 1945, and factory and warehouse stocks at end of month, August 1944, and July and August 1945

Items grouped by major use	Production		Stocks (crude basis)		
	Jan.-Aug. 1944	Jan.-Aug. 1945	Aug. 31 1944	July 31 1945	Aug. 31 1945
	Mil. lb.	Mil. lb.	Mil. lb.	Mil. lb.	Mil. lb.
Food fats and oils					
Butter 1/	1,100.7	1,045.0	137.9	184.8	206.5
Lard and rendered pork fat 2/	1,810.6	861.6	609.6	105.0	93.2
Oleo oil, edible animal stearine, and edible tallow	141.7	143.5	24.5	19.2	15.6
Total edible animal fats	3,053.0	2,050.1	772.0	309.0	315.3
Corn oil 3/	137.3	146.1	21.0	19.6	16.5
Cottonseed oil 3/	513.6	712.2	225.5	351.5	288.8
Olive oil, edible	5.5	4.3	2.0	1.8	1.8
Peanut oil 3/	77.5	79.4	44.8	51.8	49.1
Sesame oil	4/	4/	3.7	1.7	1.6
Soybean oil 3/	876.7	948.3	241.9	232.8	222.4
Total edible vegetable oils	1,610.6	1,890.3	538.9	659.2	580.2
Soap fats and oils					
Tallow, inedible	681.7	617.2	177.7	118.1	102.0
Grease, excluding wool grease	455.0	349.7	163.7	75.0	75.0
Palm oil 3/	---	---	54.1	71.2	68.0
Fish oil	75.7	66.1	109.1	60.1	78.0
Marine mammal oil	.1	---	51.7	24.8	23.3
Olive oil, inedible and foots	4/	4/	3.4	1.8	1.6
Total slow-lathering oils	1,212.5	1,033.0	559.7	351.0	347.9
Babassu oil 3/	4/	4/	5.7	11.1	13.0
Coconut oil 3/	86.9	114.3	103.5	124.4	137.4
Palm-kernel oil 3/	4/	4/	5/	6/ 27.5	6/ 29.2
Total lauric-acid oils	86.9	114.3	109.2	163.0	179.6
Drying oils					
Castor oil, dehydrated 7/	55.6	41.5	11.1	8.4	9.4
Linseed oil	704.6	281.2	323.0	145.4	151.0
Oiticica oil	4/	4/	4.6	7.7	9.0
Perilla oil	---	---	.3	.1	.1
Tung oil	4/	4/	24.6	12.9	11.9
Total drying oils	760.2	322.7	363.6	174.5	181.4
Other industrial					
Neat's-foot oil	1.5	1.6	2.5	1.9	2.1
Wool grease	11.1	11.8	3.7	2.9	3.4
Cod oil and fish-liver oils	6.5	4.2	16.0	13.3	13.8
Castor oil, No. 1 and No. 3 8/	51.5	65.6	42.6	11.9	13.5
Rape oil	---	---	15.6	18.2	21.2
Other vegetable oils	23.2	82.1	34.7	45.8	47.0
Total	93.8	165.3	115.1	94.0	101.0
Grand Total	6,816.9	5,575.7	2,458.6	1,750.7	1,705.4

Compiled from reports of the Bureau of the Census, except as noted, Data include stocks held by Government in reported positions. Totals computed from unrounded numbers.

1/ Creamery butter production and cold-storage stocks, U.S. Department of Agriculture. 2/ Federally inspected production, USDA. 3/ Stocks, crude oil plus refined oil converted to crude basis by dividing by the following factors: Babassu, corn, cottonseed, palm, and palm-kernel oils. 0.93; coconut, peanut and soybean oils, 0.94. 4/ Included in other vegetable oils. 5/ Not reported. 6/ Crude only. 7/ Converted to crude basis by dividing by 0.88. 8/ Estimated quantity used in manufacture of dehydrated castor oil excluded from production.

FOS - 104   - 15 -

Table 7.— Imports and exports of fats, oils, oil-bearing materials, and fat-and-oil products,
January-August, average 1938-41, 1944 and 1945

Primary fats

Item	Imports for consumption — Average 1938-41	1944	1945 2/	Exports — Average 1938-41	1944	1945 2/
	Mil. lb.	Mil. lb.	Mil. lb.	Mil. lb.	Mil. lb.	Mil. lb.
Animal fats						
Butter	1.1	1.7	3/	6.4	50.8	4/ 25.9
Lard	3/	3/	.2	191.6	617.1	465.1
Oleo oil	---	---	---	2.3	2.4	.2
Stearine, animal, edible	3/	---	.2	.1	---	3/
Oleo stock	---	---	---	1.6	.2	---
Tallow, edible	.6	18.8	1.7	.1	1.1	3/
Tallow, inedible	3.9	37.5	31.6	1.0	14.6	4.4
Greases	3/	3/	3/	2.7	1.9	4.3
Wool grease	1.6	3/	.6	---	---	---
Neat's-foot oil	---	.4	.6	.4	.1	.1
Total, animal	7.2	58.4	34.9	206.3	659.2	504.0
Marine fats						
Fish-liver oils	27.2	13.6	14.9	---	1.2	3.0
Fish oils	1.6	8.6	10.2	2.1	7.4	8.2
Marine mammal oils	14.2	1.5	1.6	3/	2.7	13.0
Total, marine	43.0	25.7	26.7	2.1	11.4	24.2
Vegetable fats						
Babassu oil	.3	.9	2.7	---	---	---
Cashew nut shell liquid (oil)	2.0	4.2	.2	---	---	---
Castor oil	.1	13.6	1.1	.7	1.7	.9
Coconut oil	242.2	37.3	30.7	24.1	4.9	.1
Corn oil	7.4	3/	3/	.1	.2	.1
Cottonseed oil	24.3	4.6	33.0	7.4	4.3	7.0
Japan wax (tallow)	1.7	---	---	---	---	---
Linseed oil	.1	63.9	28.9	1.9	237.6	6.4
Oiticica oil	13.6	5.0	15.1	---	---	---
Olive oil, edible	36.0	.2	8.7	---	.1	.1
Olive-oil "foots"	14.3	---	---	---	.4	.1
Olive oil, inedible	3.3	.1	---	---	3/	3/
Palm-kernel oil	1.1	---	---	---	---	---
Palm oil	180.5	39.9	53.9	12.2	4.2	14.6
Peanut oil	3.3	3/	---	2.0	.2	.1
Perilla oil	16.2	---	---	---	3/	---
Rape oil	7.1	13.0	17.7	---	.2	.5
Sesame oil	2.2	.9	---	---	---	---
Soybean oil	1.9	.1	.57	7.7	32.1	28.4
Sunflower oil	.1	33.2	57.6	5/	5/	39.0
Teaseed oil	3.2	---	---	---	---	---
Tung oil	59.3	1.8	---	2.9	.1	1.5
Vegetable tallow	1.1	3/	.2	---	---	---
Other vegetable oils and fats	---	1.0	1.1	6/10.2	10.4	2.1
Vegetable oils, shipments to U. S. territories	---	---	---	6/ 6.2	6.5	6.0
Total, vegetable	621.2	219.7	252.1	75.5	303.0	109.9
Total, primary fats	671.4	303.9	313.7	283.9	1,002.5	634.1

Oil-bearing materials (in terms of oil)

Item	Average 1938-41	1944	1945 2/	Exports Average 1938-41	1944	1945 2/
Babassu kernels (63 percent)	37.5	4.8	63.6	---	---	---
Castor beans (45 percent)	64.7	104.2	97.7	---	---	---
Copra (63 percent)	219.1	75.2	114.0	13.8	---	---
Cottonseed (15.5 percent)	---	---	3/	---	.5	1.0
Flaxseed (34 percent)	198.7	173.0	53.2	---	.5	3/
Murumuru kernels (36 percent) 7/	.9	.4	.3	---	---	---
Palm-nut kernels (45 percent)	6.0	8.8	36.3	---	---	---
Peanuts, shelled (39 percent)	---	---	19.6	---	---	---
Perilla seed (37 percent)	.6	---	---	---	---	---
Sesame seed (47 percent)	3.1	3.4	3/	---	---	---
Soybeans (15 percent)	---	---	---	9.9	3.5	38.3
Tucum kernels (43 percent)	2.4	.7	3.9	---	---	---
Total, oil-bearing materials	533.0	370.5	368.5	23.7	4.4	39.3

Manufactured products (fat content)

Item	Average 1938-41	1944	1945 2/	Exports Average 1938-41	1944	1945 2/
Margarine 8/	6/ 1.2	---	---	6/ 1.0	41.8	44.9
Shortening	6/ .9	3/	3/	6/ 5.6	10.4	15.9
Soap	6/ 2.0	.5	.2	6/20.9	20.5	37.1
Total, manufactured products	4.1	.5	.2	27.5	72.7	97.9

Grand total

Item	Average 1938-41	1944	1945 2/	Exports Average 1938-41	1944	1945 2/
All items	1,208.4	674.6	672.5	335.1	1,079.6	771.3

Compiled from Monthly Summary of Foreign Commerce of the United States, records of the Bureau of the Census, and reports of the U. S. Department of Agriculture. Totals computed from unrounded numbers.

The following items are not included above: Procurement by the Army in 1945 for European relief, 65 million pounds of lard and 6 million pounds fat content of soap. Procurement of margarine, shortening, and soap by the American Red Cross in terms of fat content, 14 million pounds in 1944 and 10 million pounds in 1945.

1/ Includes shipments to U. S. territories of butter, lard, and manufactured products; reexports of coconut, palm, and tung oils, olive-oil foots, and copra; and reexports in 1944 and 1945 of certain quantities of whale oil and sunflower oil reported in imports for consumption. Shipments include special programs of USDA in 1944 and 1945. 2/ Preliminary. 3/ Less than 50,000 pounds. 4/ Includes actual weight of butter oil and spreads (Army). These were not reported separately prior to 1945. 5/ Not reported separately. 6/ Eight-twelfths of annual average. 7/ 1938-41, 35 percent. 8/ Imported margarine goes largely to Puerto Rico and the Virgin Islands.

Table 8.—Fats and oils: Total factory production, January-August 1944 and 1945, and factory and warehouse stocks at end of month, August 1944, and July and August 1945

Items grouped by major use	Production		Stocks (crude basis)		
	Jan.-Aug. 1944	Jan.-Aug. 1945	Aug. 31 1944	July 31 1945	Aug. 31 1945
	Mil. lb.	Mil. lb.	Mil. lb.	Mil. lb.	Mil. lb.
Food fats and oils					
Butter 1/ ....:	1,100.7	1,045.0	137.9	184.8	206.5
Lard and rendered pork fat 2/ .:	1,810.6	861.6	609.6	105.0	93.2
Oleo oil, edible animal stear- ine, and edible tallow ....:	141.7	143.5	24.5	19.2	15.6
Total edible animal fats ...:	3,053.0	2,050.1	772.0	309.0	315.3
Corn oil 3/ ....:	137.3	146.1	21.0	19.6	16.5
Cottonseed oil 3/ ....:	513.6	712.2	225.5	351.5	288.8
Olive oil, edible ....:	5.5	4.3	2.0	1.8	1.8
Peanut oil 3/ ....:	77.5	79.4	44.8	51.8	49.1
Sesame oil ....:	4/	4/	3.7	1.7	1.6
Soybean oil 3/ ....:	876.7	948.3	241.9	232.8	222.4
Total edible vegetable oils :	1,610.6	1,890.3	538.9	659.2	580.2
Soap fats and oils					
Tallow, inedible ....:	681.7	617.2	177.7	118.1	102.0
Grease, excluding wool grease .:	455.0	349.7	163.7	75.0	75.0
Palm oil 3/ ....:	----	----	54.1	71.2	68.0
Fish oil ....:	75.7	66.1	109.1	60.1	78.0
Marine mammal oil ....:	.1	----	51.7	24.8	23.3
Olive oil, inedible and foots :	4/	4/	3.4	1.8	1.6
Total slow-lathering oils ..:	1,212.5	1,033.0	559.7	351.0	347.9
Babassu oil 3/ ....:	4/	4/	5.7	11.1	13.0
Coconut oil 3/ ....:	86.9	114.3	103.5	124.4	137.4
Palm-kernel oil 3/ ....:	4/	4/	5/	6/ 27.5	6/ 29.2
Total lauric-acid oils .....:	86.9	114.3	109.2	163.0	179.6
Drying oils					
Castor oil, dehydrated 7/ ...:	55.6	41.5	11.1	8.4	9.4
Linseed oil ....:	704.6	281.2	323.0	145.4	151.0
Oiticica oil ....:	4/	4/	4.6	7.7	9.0
Perilla oil ....:	----	----	.3	.1	.1
Tung oil ....:	4/	4/	24.6	12.9	11.9
Total drying oils ....:	760.2	322.7	363.6	174.5	181.4
Other industrial					
Neat's-foot oil ....:	1.5	1.6	2.5	1.9	2.1
Wool grease ....:	11.1	11.8	3.7	2.9	3.4
Cod oil and fish-liver oils ...:	6.5	4.2	16.0	13.3	13.8
Castor oil, No. 1 and No. 3 8/ :	51.5	65.6	42.6	11.9	13.5
Rape oil ....:	----	----	15.6	18.2	21.2
Other vegetable oils ....:	23.2	82.1	34.7	45.8	47.0
Total ....:	93.8	165.3	115.1	94.0	101.0
Grand Total.............:	6,816.9	5,575.7	2,458.6	1,750.7	1,705.4

Compiled from reports of the Bureau of the Census, except as noted, Data include stocks held by Government in reported positions. Totals computed from unrounded numbers.
1/ Creamery butter production and cold-storage stocks, U.S. Department of Agriculture. 2/ Federally inspected production, USDA. 3/ Stocks, crude oil plus refined oil converted to crude basis by dividing by the following factors: Babassu, corn, cottonseed, palm, and palm-kernel oils. 0.93; coconut, peanut and soybean oils, 0.94. 4/ Included in other vegetable oils. 5/ Not reported. 6/ Crude only. 7/ Converted to crude basis by dividing by 0.88. 8/ Estimated quantity used in manufacture of dehydrated castor oil excluded from production.

Table 9.- Price received by farmers and prices at terminal
markets for specified oil-bearing materials and oilmeals
October 1943 and 1944, August-October 1945

Oilseeds

Item	Unit	October		1945		
		1943	1944	Aug.	Sept.	Oct.
		Dollars	Dollars	Dollars	Dollars	Dollars
Castor beans, Brazilian, f.o.b. Brazilian ports ......:	Long ton :	75.00	61.00	82.50	82.50	84.50
Cottonseed, United States average ....:	Short ton :	52.50	52.70	52.50	51.40	51.00
Flaxseed, No. 1, Minneapolis .:	Bushel :	2.99	3.10	3.10	3.10	3.10
Flaxseed, United States average ....:	Bushel :	2.79	2.90	2.89	2.89	2.89
Peanuts, No. 1 shelled, Spanish, Southeastern shipping points ....:	100 pounds:	14.00	14.25	14.25	14.25	14.25
Peanuts, United States average ....:	100 pounds:	7.05	7.71	8.19	8.29	8.06
Soybeans, No. 2 Yellow, Chicago ...:...............:	Bushel :	1.83	2.04	2.18	2.17	2.11
Soybeans, United States average ....:...............:	Bushel :	1.80	2.04	2.12	2.07	2.06
		Oilseed Meals 1/				
Copra meal, Los Angeles ......:	Short ton :	51.50	49.80	2/50.00	2/49.50	2/49.50
Cottonseed meal, 41 percent protein, Memphis ....:	" " :	48.50	48.50	48.75	48.75	48.75
Cottonseed meal, 41 percent protein, Chicago ....:	" " :	54.45	54.45	54.75	54.75	54.75
Linseed meal, 32 percent protein, Minneapolis ....:	" " :	45.50	45.50	45.50	45.50	45.50
Linseed meal, 34 percent protein, New York ....:	" " :	2/49.00	2/49.00	49.00	49.00	49.00
Peanut meal, 45 percent protein, f.o.b. South-eastern mills ....:	" " :	53.00	53.00	53.00	53.00	53.00
Soybean meal, 41 percent protein, Chicago ...:.......:	" " :	51.90	52.00	52.00	52.00	52.00

Compiled from Oil, Paint and Drug Reporter, Daily Market Record (Minneapolis),
Chicago Journal of Commerce, reports of the Bureau of Agricultural Economics,
and records of Production and Marketing Administration.
1/ Bagged, carlots.
2/ Original quotation adjusted to bagged-carlots basis.

Lightning Source UK Ltd.
Milton Keynes UK
UKHW021502030219
336610UK00006B/89/P